11

Hiro Mashima

Translated and adapted by William Flanagan
Lettered by North Market Street Graphics

Ballantine Books · New York

A Del Rey Manga/Kodansha Trade Paperback Original

Fairy Tail volume 11 copyright © 2008 Hiro Mashima
English translation copyright © 2010 Hiro Mashima

Published in the United States by Del Rey, an imprint of The Random House Publishing Group, a division of Random House, Inc., New York.

DEL REY is a registered trademark and the Del Rey colophon is a trademark of Random House, Inc.

Publication rights arranged through Kodansha Ltd.

First published in Japan in 2008 by Kodansha Ltd., Tokyo

ISBN 978-0-345-51992-4

Printed in the United States of America

www.delreymanga.com

9 8 7 6 5 4 3 2 1

Translator/Adapter: William Flanagan
Lettering: North Market Street Graphics

Contents

7/10

My name is Tama
Gonzaburo!!
I'm going to slide right
down your throat!!
And just think how tasty
your beef bowl would be
with me on top!!
Can you even imagine
breakfast without me?!
Wow-wow!! I'm a
reproductive cell!!...
Sorry.
I'm really tired.

—Hiro Mashima

Honorifics Explained

Throughout the Del Rey Manga books, you will find Japanese honorifics left intact in the translations. For those not familiar with how the Japanese use honorifics and, more important, how they differ from American honorifics, we present this brief overview.

Politeness has always been a critical facet of Japanese culture. Ever since the feudal era, when Japan was a highly stratified society, use of honorifics—which can be defined as polite speech that indicates relationship or status—has played an essential role in the Japanese language. When addressing someone in Japanese, an honorific usually takes the form of a suffix attached to one's name (example: "Asuna-san"), is used as a title at the end of one's name, or appears in place of the name itself (example: "Negi-sensei," or simply "Sensei").

Honorifics can be expressions of respect or endearment. In the context of manga and anime, honorifics give insight into the nature of the relationship between characters. Many English translations leave out these important honorifics and therefore distort the feel of the original Japanese. Because Japanese honorifics contain nuances that English honorifics lack, it is our policy at Del Rey not to translate them. Here, instead, is a guide to some of the honorifics you may encounter in Del Rey Manga.

-san: This is the most common honorific and is equivalent to Mr., Miss, Ms., or Mrs. It is the all-purpose honorific and can be used in any situation where politeness is required.

-sama: This is one level higher than "-san" and is used to confer great respect.

-dono: This comes from the word "tono," which means "lord." It is an even higher level than "-sama" and confers utmost respect.

-kun: This suffix is used at the end of boys' names to express familiarity or endearment. It is also sometimes used by men among friends, or when addressing someone younger or of a lower station.

-chan: This is used to express endearment, mostly toward girls. It is also used for little boys, pets, and even between lovers. It gives a sense of childish cuteness.

Bozu: This is an informal way to refer to a boy, similar to the English terms "kid" and "squirt."

Sempai/
Senpai: This title suggests that the addressee is one's senior in a group or organization. It is most often used in a school setting, where underclassmen refer to their upperclassmen as "sempai." It can also be used in the workplace, such as when a newer employee addresses an employee who has seniority in the company.

Kohai: This is the opposite of "sempai" and is used toward underclassmen in school or newcomers in the workplace. It connotes that the addressee is of a lower station.

Sensei: Literally meaning "one who has come before," this title is used for teachers, doctors, or masters of any profession or art.

-[blank]: This is usually forgotten in these lists, but it is perhaps the most significant difference between Japanese and English. The lack of honorific means that the speaker has permission to address the person in a very intimate way. Usually, only family, spouses, or very close friends have this kind of permission. Known as *yobisute*, it can be gratifying when someone who has earned the intimacy starts to call one by one's name without an honorific. But when that intimacy hasn't been earned, it can be very insulting.

FAIRY TAIL

11

HIRO MASHIMA

CONTENTS

FAIRY TAIL

Chapter 83: Find the Way

Every living being within that tower will be wiped out!!

That includes any humans in the area!

Everything that falls under the Etherion attack is rendered "null"!

This is to protect the entire magic world!

It is a price we must pay!

In a manner of speaking, we ourselves will be one of those sacrifices.

Elder Belno!!

SKRRT

Elder Leiji!! If we make an unannounced attack on Ka-Elm national soil, history will record *our names* on the list of mass murderers!!!

It is exactly as Sieg says. We live now only because others have previously sacrificed their lives. The history of magic proves that over and over.

CHATTER

What?!!

I see no alternative! I agree to use Etherion.

We must say that to the children when we teach them of the sanctity of human life!

"The dead cannot be brought back to life!"

CHATTER

Only one more vote... hm?

We need only one more vote!!

No...just talking to myself.

Did you say something, Jellal-sama?

Sir?

6

Only one more until game over.

Heh heh heh...

Yes... The most evil black magician in the history of the magic world. The legendary black wizard.

That Zeref that you mentioned...

Wait a second, Erza...

That isn't all. It's probably that Deliora is also a demon from the Book of Zeref.

Wh-When the demon came out of Lullaby, didn't somebody say something about the Book of Zeref?

!!!

So Jellal is trying to revive this Zeref?

They say that Zeref had enough magic power to easily create frightening creatures like those.

Shô...

According to the words of some of my old friends, the moment that Zeref is revived, then Heaven will be in control of everything.

I don't understand his motive.

They were saying that you betrayed them, Erza...

...but wasn't it really Jellal who betrayed them?

Now that you mention it, there's one thing I don't understand about your old friends.

However, I abandoned them for eight years.

There is little difference between that and a direct betrayal.

Perhaps he did some sort of indoctrination on them after he expelled me from the Tower of Heaven.

9

But that's only because Jellal threatened your friends' lives if you ever even got close!!

And even then, he—

If I am able to defeat Jellal, then it will all be over.

That's enough, Lucy.

SHK

...will mean that the outside world will never hear from me again.

This battle... ...win or lose...

For some reason, those words keep coming back to me.

I wonder if that's really true.

10

Don't make me laugh!!! The truth is the exact opposite!!!

You think you can win a little sympathy from your friends with that load of bull?!!

Eight years ago you set a bomb on the ship we were trying to escape in, and you ran away by yourself!!!

If Jellal hadn't figured out your treason and come to warn us, none of us would have made it out alive!!!

And that Sis had become drunk with magic power and had decided to throw away her past, including us!!!

He said that "magic" was the road to salvation, and any unbelievers would be swept away by fate!!!

Jellal told us everything!!!

Do you think the Erza you used to know could ever do something like that?

Jellal...

...told you?

Wh-What do you guys know?!!

You know nothing about us!!!

That's why we spent eight years finishing this tower!!!

It was all for Jellal's sake!!!!

We were saved by Jellal's words!!!!

Y-You wanted to fool us?!

My plan was to put you unconscious in order to fool Shô and the others into thinking you were dead, but since it was just an ice decoy, then I knew I could make a show of it.

I never intended to kill anyone.

I believed in you from the start, Erza.

SKRCH
SKRCHI
TO
TO

Simon, you...

I had to wait for my chance, so I pretended to be fooled too.

You, Wally, Millianna—you've all been tricked by Jellal.

· · ·

And continued to believe for these eight years.

I was so happy to see you, Erza.

From the bottom of my heart.

GAMPH

Simon...

Why wasn't I...

...able to trust my sister too?!

Why? Why does everybody trust Sis so much?

Why?!

We are going to fight Jellal.

We are going to combine our strengths.

And our first step is to prevent Wally and the Salamander from taking each other out.

I think it's stuck!

Huh?

Well, who cares? As long as it's fun!

Aww!! I give up!!

22

Chapter 84:
Natsu-Cat Fight!!

Wait a minute...I think Lucy would give us a better reaction, huh?

And while I'm at it, I'll give Erza a little shock too!

Eh heh heh! Happy will be so surprised by this!!

CHAK

The end! Get it, boy?

KACHIK

...back then, it wouldn't have been too far of a stretch for Natsu or Lucy to have been killed.

Say...Do you think...we can really trust that guy?

Okay, he didn't try to kill us. I'll give you that, but...

...that Natsu wouldn't die!!

Besides, I truly believed...

Um...And your beliefs about me...?

But if those wizards would have died due to attacks on that small scale, then they have no chance fighting Jellal.

I don't intend to give you any excuses.

You heard me...

You people have yet to notice Natsu's true power!

DONE DEAL

DO WHLINK

THLINNK

How long do you intend to wear that?

I can't get it off!!!

Yeah!! I got my revenge on Boxy!!!

THUNK

THUNK

38

HEH

They've had their turn. Now it's mine, don't you think?

TONK TONK TONK

Are you sure?

KRAKL

KRAKL

KRAKL

KRAKL

LIWOOOOHH

WHOOSH

Hahn!!!

Hell!!! I'll show them the best of the worst of Hell!!!!

BLUUN

Go to Hell!!!!

Assassin's Guild Death's Head Caucus: **Vidaldus Taka**

Hoo-Hoot.

Assassin's Guild Death's Head Caucus: **Fukuro**

Love and life are doomed to fail.

This evening, we celebrate!

Assassin's Guild, Death's Head Caucus Squad Leader: Special Guerilla Squad: **Ikaruga**

Chapter 85: Heaven's Game

44

It's off!!!

Unh...

What kind of head hole does that mask have?!

AH HA HA

Now it's stuck on Boxy!!

Eh?

ZUPOP

CAT

SLUMP

Uhn...

THWONK

WOBBLE

Our match isn't finished yet, Salamander!!

45

We're going to Heaven...

You did a number on me. I paid you back.

Now that I know that both Erza and Happy are okay, there's no point in going on with this.

YEAH YEAH
うん

...can be found in a world, where we control everybody else...

Jellal told us that true freedom...

MWUUP
MWUUP

MWUUP
MWUUP

BWAAM

BWAAM

MWUUP

Mouths? Coming out of every-

What is this, Natsu?! It's pretty creepy!!

There is a very real chance that the Council will attack this tower with a satellite square.

Finally, allow me to explain one extra-special rule.

That would be their extremely effective, wide-area destruction magic, Etherion.

It gets me high to be in the middle of the most dangerous job in the world!!!!

No!!! Reverse it!!! Just the opposite!!!!

Vidaldus-han? Do I sense cowardice?

ケス... TEEHEE

If that comes down, then we're all going straight to Hell!!!!

Jellal, you ass!!! You never told us about this!!!

...everyone will die.

That means the game ends without a winner.

But the moment Etherion comes down...

There's no telling how much time we have left.

52

I'd imagine he's at the very top.

Well, that fires me up!!!

...all we've got to do is take out this Jellal guy, and it's over, right?

I don't get any of this, but...

All I wanted was true freedom!

If we get hit with that, we all die?!

Wh-What is this, Jellal? The Etherion thing?

I don't know what brand of freedom you're looking for...

...but Fairy Tail gives a guy a lot of freedom, and it's really fun!!

The Justice Knight, Fukuro, has come!!!

Hoo-Hoo!!!

I will tolerate no breaking of the rules!!!

Th-That's...?!!

!!!

A bird!!! A bird just said something about justice!!!

Don't even try to get in a fight with that guy!!!

Natsu!!! That guy... is friends with the boxy guy!!!

This is bad!!! Come with me!!!

?!

Right now, I'm on your side!!!

The Death's Head Caucus of the Assassin's Guild!!!!

Th-That's how strong they are...

It is one of the dark guilds.

It's the worst kind of guild!!! They don't even take normal jobs anymore, now that they specialize in assassinations!!

Assassin's Guild?!!

They are professional killers!!! You mustn't fight them!!!!

Hoo-Hoo! Evil must be destroyed!!

And inside the guild is a three-man team called the Trinity Raven!! Legend has it that in the Cabria War, the three of them alone murdered all of the commissioned officers in the western army!!!

Oh, no!!!

So he's one of those three people... er...three birds?

FAIRY TAIL

Chapter 86: Rock of Succubus

Do they... commit murders as a business?

No, Sala-mander!!! Don't!!!

Don't even try to approach the assassin's guild!!!

It's that kind of business itself that I can't stand!!

And I really don't like how they call it a "guild"!!!

I don't even like that there are clients for jobs like that!!

GWOOO

You're pitiful, Simon. You're out just as the game is beginning.

KALUNK!!

GONK

Next, it's Fukuro versus.... Natsu Dragneel.

Hmm...I would have liked Natsu to have come and faced me, but...

...it looks like he won't have the chance.

TOK!!

TOK!!

Natsu!!!

Natsu-san!!!

True. If he is anything like Gajeel-kun, his nose should be very good as well.

He's got pretty good ears, so he should be able to hear us from a good distance away.

We had no choice.

Juvia wonders why she is stuck looking for Natsu-san with Lucy-san.

You're ignoring me?

You put "-kun" at the end of Gajeel's name?

I can't stop worrying about Erza. I'm going to go after that Shô guy.

I'm leaving the search for Natsu to you two!!

JAANNN

!!!!

I'm putting "That has nothing to do with me" on full power here!! Let's try to get along, okay?

However, leaving two rivals in love alone like this. I wonder what kind of bloodbath he expected to come back to?

Yes, if Gray-sama ordered it, then we did have no choice but to obey.

JANN
JAANN
JANN
JANN

Juvia thinks the guitar player is very skillful.

Whatever it is, it's too loud!!!

JA-JAAN

You are!! You're ignoring me!!!

JAAN

JAANN

Wh-What is that sound?!!

A guitar?!!

JAAAANNN

Rock ?!!

You're a rocker too?!!

GYA HA GLUB GLUB GLUB GLUB

SHHHH

Water Lock!!!!

Well, that's a former Element 4 for you!! I'm glad you're not my enemy!

He is all talk.

GLOOG

In a very creepy way!!!

SHWR SHWR

Juvia's Water Lock...

...vanished?!!

You...How did you defeat my Water Lock?!

A good wash with lots of water gets the bed-head out of your hair!!

But don't shampoo every morning since that causes damage!!

But I never use alcohol or oils on it!! They damage the luster!!

My hair can suck up any liquid matter!!

Have I told you girls yet how good you look?!

Heh heh!

You're kid- ding...

Water... can't affect him?

It's going to be...

...to send to the devil... But which one shall I choose...

SWIP SWIP SWIP

Here it is again!! The usual!!

Wh-What are you saying?

Whenever they call you cute, it's the start of trouble!!

FAIRY TAIL

Chapter 87: Lucy vs. Juvia

KRIKK

Those little girls...

...are doing a magic fusion?!

SST

SHIVER

Th-This kind of magic power...

What?!

H-Hey!!! You're sending me more than I can take...

No!!!

Wait a second!!!

What's with all this water?!!

SHEEEN

Juvia is back to normal!!!!

We did it!!!!

She's scary...

I-I'm sorry...

What's next, summoning me from toilet water?!! Because if you do, you're dead!!!

!!!

Look at the way you summoned me to this dismal place!!!

Chapter 88: Natsu Becomes a Meal

I'm leaving this minute for a two-week trip with my boyfriend. Don't you dare call on me!!

Say you agree!!!

Lucy-san, love is very important.

Just leave me alone!!!

Not possible, but...

You should find yourself a boyfriend too, and soon!!!

I agree.

Anyway...

104

We just took down one of those knights!!

It isn't going the way that Jellal planned!!!

We both did!

No. The one who took him down is Lucy-san.

You don't have to add the "-san" with me!!

I mean, we're friends now, aren't we?

Back then, you called out "Lucy!!"

I got the feeling we could be friends. It made me happy!

AH HA HA!!
That's a funny
way of saying
it!!

Eh?

Juvia...is
dropping
water from
her eyes!!

SNIFF

But, man,
did that fight
completely
exhaust
me!!!

Juvia
too.

...but it's said he was never able to achieve it.

I've heard of a monk who spent his life preparing himself to do a Unison Raid...

They did a Unison Raid?

Heh heh!

They may be nothing more than young girls, but they are worthy of being Erza's companions.

It might not have been intentional, but they achieved something incredible.

Then I'll just move another piece forward on the board.

Era...

...stands at four in favor and five against.

Thus with the votes cast, we rule against the use of Etherion.

The decision to use an Etherion attack against the Tower of Heaven...

There is a path to peaceful resolution that doesn't resort to bloodshed.

Don't embarrass yourself, Sieg. You've lectured us quite enough.

Wait!!!

You people don't understand the true situation yet!!!

Jellal is trying to revive a dead man!!!!

...history is being made without you!!!

Peace?! You're pursuing that ridiculous waste of time, and meanwhile...

Don't you even feel it?

It's too early for an attack!

First of all, we don't even know if the R-System works!!

. . . .

Sieg, what are you...

What was that?

The overwhelming amount of negative magical power?! The fear that is caused by the man he is trying to bring back to life?!

The Black
Wizard
Zeref!!!!

I knew the information would raise baseless doubts, so I kept my silence!

What I want to know is how you know this, Sieg?!!

S-Sieg, you...What did you just...

And I know what he is trying to accomplish!!!

But I know this man Jellal!!

Sieg...You'd better tell us everything!!

!!!!

CHATTER

*Fire Dragon's Talon!

Wait!!!

Hey!!!

GULP

What do you think you're doing?!!!

Those who I devour, I digest their magic!!

He swallowed him whole...?!!

Hoo-Hoo!!

We have eight yea votes, and one nay.

And so...

Is...this why the Assassin's Guild is so scary?

...the motion to use Etherion against the Tower of Heaven is passed!

I wash my hands of the whole thing.

Be sure you take responsibility for the outcome.

...but you can at least accept that we can't allow Zeref to be brought back to life, right?

Yajima-san...You may not be able to understand this...

Of course! I accept full responsibility for the use.

What I'm talking about is responsibility for human lives!!!!

You are going to live with the weight of lost human lives on your back, Sieg!!!!

TWRL

You'll have your answer to that in a few moments.

Etherion will launch its attack in one hour!!!

Everyone make your preparations!!!

Now...What will you do? There's no time left!

The light will fall any time now!!!

Erza... You've lost your very best piece.

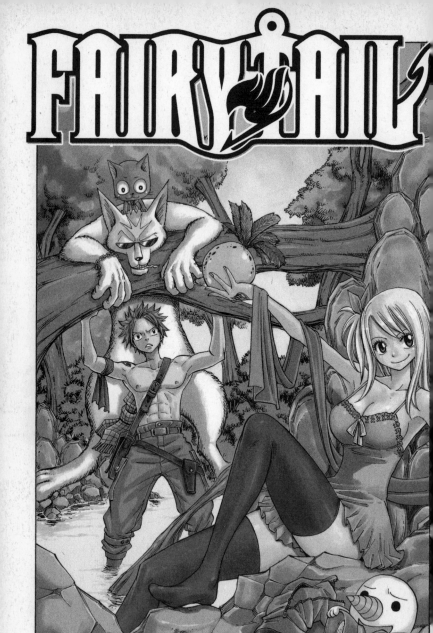

FAIRY TAIL

Chapter 89: Armor Around a Heart

Then get going again!!! If we don't find Erza, we're in trouble, right?!!!

I was stopped...

GLARE

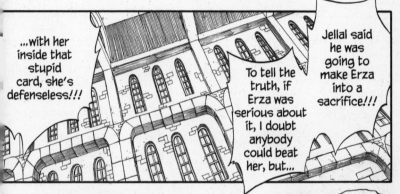

...with her inside that stupid card, she's defenseless!!!

To tell the truth, if Erza was serious about it, I doubt anybody could beat her, but...

Jellal said he was going to make Erza into a sacrifice!!!

What?

Gray...Natsu was...eaten by that guy over there...

I know the timing of when we told Shô the truth was a mistake...

...but I never imagined he'd go off and do that.

I've got no time to stand around here playing games with some jerk like you!!!!

Erza-sama!! The one fated to carry Fairy Tail on her shoulders!!!

But I never thought that Erza could work "the great Gray" over like that!! Impressive!!

Shut up!!!

You don't quit!! Are you in love with her or something?

Did Erza get the best of you again, Gray?

Erza has to be in Fairy Tail!!!

So that she doesn't have to cry again!!!!

GAKUUN

FAIRY TAIL

Chapter 90: Ikaruga

HOO...
HOO

HAHH

HAHH

HAHH

HAHH

Gray Fullbuster... He's far stronger than the information I gathered gave him credit for.

Hurry... We've got...

...to find... Erza...

WOBBLE

Kh...

Natsu!! Wake up...

The world is spinning...

Or maybe... his feelings for his comrades gave his magic a huge boost?

You managed to get yourself into a very good guild.

Erza...

When we're shooting the devil, we aim Etherion and pray!! That's all we can do!!

It's Zeref!! The devil himself!!

The time is almost here.

Sieg-sama.

Your eight-year plan is coming to reality.

I will always trust you, Sieg-sama.

No. Not even slightly.

Doesn't it scare you, Ultear?

But I feel myself trembling.

That's true.

HEE HEE

I imagine so, hm? After all, *there is no risk to your life.*

!!!

If he fails, he dies?

However, it's well worth betting one's life on.

VLITT

If I fail, I die.

Since I'm creating my ideal!!

Yes.

Jellal!!

Dammit!!!

Damn you!!!!

You're fine now, Sis!! I'll protect you!!!

Shô!!!

Listen to me!!! Just calm down!!!

And get me out of here!!!

You did a thorough job making a fool of me, didn't you?!!

Shô!!

You hurt Sis!!!

FLIPP

!

WHUDD

When could she have...

Oh my! Is *that* where you were hiding?

Erza-han!

Sis...

Shô!!!

Don't worry... That card will protect you...

Nothing from the outside can hurt you!

Get me out of here now!!!

She isn't somebody you can beat!!!

Your attacks put a strain on the spatial confinement.

You cut me out of the card.

That was so wonderful, I can't find the words.

...that Sis could use that to her advantage... Sis is amazing!

I'm shocked that there's a sword that can cut through alternate space, but...

!!!

PAKIK
PAKIK
PAKIK

PAKIK

HEE

I have no use for you. Leave!

Consider that my greeting to you.

Oh my! It couldn't be that you didn't see it coming, could it?

Kah!!!

PA-CHAM

PA-CHAM

PA-CHAM

KLAKK

CLUNK

KRUMBL

KRUMBL

KLATTER

Chapter 91:
One Woman! The Decisive Outfit

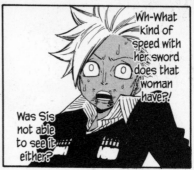

Wh-What kind of speed with her sword does that woman have?!

Was Sis not able to see it either?

166

DO WHAMM

Do I detect armor with protection against fire?

I compliment you on your speed donning it.

I'm afraid that outfit will never do when standing before his lordship.

I feel it is time you donned your best armor, wouldn't you say?

BAA

Uwaah!!

CHAKL

Just cloth?!!

It is nothing but cloth.

Whatever can be the meaning of that getup? I sense no magic coming from your outfit.

I am not strong at all.

Sis!!! You're stronger than this, right?!!

Sis, what are you doing?!! You should have tons of strong armor left to wear!!!

And here I was kind enough to show you my sword skills...

TWITCH

...but you go so far as to mock me?!!

Okay, but you're alone now. What are you crying for?!

Not strong...

I like being alone.

It's when I'm with other people that I feel uneasy.

Too many of my friends have died right before my eyes.

And...

I haven't even been able to protect those I consider precious.

······

I'm not crying!

I'm always crying.

I shut my own heart within armor...

...and inside, I cried.

Stronger.

I always wanted everyone to see me getting stronger and stronger.

I'm weak!!! That's why I'm always hiding inside my armor!!!

I wasn't able to take it off!!!

It doesn't matter if my opponent is armored or nude.

My blade will cut.

I wanted to believe that my armor would protect me!!

But I was wrong!!!

...was get in the way of what connects one human heart to another!!!

All my armor actually did...

TAIL D'ART

The *Fairy Tail* Guild d'Art is an explosion of fan art! Please send in your black-and-white art on large postcard stock!! ♪ Those chosen to be published will get a signed mini poster! ♪ Make sure you write your real name and address on the back of your postcard!

▶ Ohh!! There's a dragon coming out of that fire!! Now that's hot!

...kuoka Prefecture, Keel

▶ Thank you!! And I love anybody who can draw such a cute Lucy!!

I love you ♥ Lucy

Virgo

Nagasaki Prefecture, Yū

▶ Now, how is it going to turn out between these two....?

Jellal & Erza

fairytail

Kanagawa Prefecture, Kirin

Reki

▶ Loke will show up again! Message to his fans, look for him!

...ate Prefecture, Yurie Abe

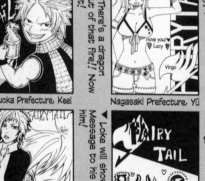

FAIRY TAIL

▶ This is a very rare pairing... I like the face Cancer is making!

I love these two!!

Cancer

Hyogo Prefecture, Mitsunari Kawabata

▶ Now that's an amazingly girlish picture of Erza!! That doesn't look very much like her, Mashima-sensei, keep up the great work!

I'm Erza of Fairy Tail. Sorry that it doesn't look very much like her.

Saitama Prefecture, Haruka

▶ Yes, who is the heroine? That is the question? I vote for Tomeko! Heh heh...

猫竜
Kittymander

▶ Kittymander...Breathes fire... Is this really now Kittymander should be drawn?!

GWOOGH

...oshima Prefecture, Momiji

Mashima-sensei, Keep up the great work! I'm rooting for you! I've been worrying ever since your last series!

▶ Kittymander...Breathes fire... Is this really now Kittymander should be drawn?!

I like Mirajane and Lucy, but my favorite is Erza!

Mirajane

Gunma Prefecture, Umi

Lucy   Erza

Tomeko

Which one is the heroine?

Fairy Tail is ♥ the best!!♥

▶ A very sexy Mira-chan! She hasn't had much of a part recently...

Kanagawa Prefecture, M.I.

FAIRY
GUILD

Okinawa Prefecture, Akemi Teruya

▲ This is pretty messed up, huh? There are people kicking things out there! (laughs)

Rejection Corner

▼ That's a pretty good dandy! Hang in there, Wally!

Hyogo Prefecture, Misaki

Send to DEL REY MANGA
Hiro Mashima
1745 Broadway
New York, NY 10019

delreymanga@randomhouse.com

Saga Prefecture, Shūichiro Iwasaki

▲ Wakaba!! You're always looking weathered. Charge!! Down the path to middle-agedness!

● Any ●
letters and postcards you send means that your personal information, such as your name, address, postal code, and other information, you include will be handed over, as is, to the author. When you send mail, please keep that in mind.

Aichi Prefecture, Takuya Takigawa

▲ postcard from fans who are rooting for Laxus!!

cuter and more erotic than the way I drew it!

Aichi Prefecture, Anzu

I'm a pro, and I throw up my hands in surrender!

Kagoshima Prefecture, Mugen

Mira: Let's continue with the next question.

Could you let me know the order from strongest to weakest of Lucy's Twelve Golden Gate Celestial Spirits?

Lucy: Ehh? That's a hard question! Celestial spirits have all sorts of different strengths and weaknesses. Hm...

Mira: Okay, after reading all the volumes so far, I'll give you my impressions.

#1. Plue (Seems to be unrivaled)
#2. Aquarius (Strong!)
#3. Loke (Sort of strong)
#4. The cow and the crab, and the others.

 : That's awful!!! Plue's not even a celestial spirit of the Twelve Golden Gates!!

 : Eh? I thought my assessment was pretty accurate.

Lucy: Not only that, but actually Taurus (Bull) and Cancer (Crab) are both pretty strong!

Mira: What about the maid and the horse guy?

 : They're really strong too!! Anyway, I can't decide an order!!

Mira: Then we'll just go on to the final question.

Why did Wally turn into that boxy guy?

Lucy: Hmm...
Mira: I wonder...
Lucy: Maybe he was pursuing being the perfect dandy, and he just turned out that way.
Mira: I've known it to happen.
Lucy: Or maybe he was going down a boxy-like passageway and by the end, he was boxy too.
Mira: Happens all the time.
Lucy: Or maybe one day, a goddess appeared before his eyes. And she ordered him to be boxy from that moment on.
Mira: Nope. That would never happen.

 : What's with the sudden rejection?

 : I think it was love.

Lucy: L-Love?

 : Isn't that how the old saying goes? "Love makes you boxy"?

 : *Nobody has ever said that!!!*

Emergency Request
Explain the Mysteries of...

FAIRYTAIL↳

From the Counter at Fairy Tail...

 : Hi everybody! Long time, no see!!

 : We were only absent from one volume.

Lucy: Honestly! When this corner was left out of the last volume, I was shocked! I thought it was all over for us!!

Mira: It can't end like that! There's still so much for readers to complain about in this manga!

Lucy: I don't know whether to be happy or sad about that! (sweat, sweat)

Mira: Let's get to the first question.

I think Lucy's hairstyle is cute, and I'd like to do the same with my hair. How do I do it?

 : Well! ♥ What a wonderful question!

Mira: It's from a grade-school-aged girl.

Lucy: Okay, let me teach you a simple way of doing it.

Complete!

First, I part my hair somewhere about one quarter of the way across the bangs. But you can do it wherever you like, really.

You want to take up some of your hair from a line above the nape of the neck, and be sure to leave some behind. You want to gather it and tie it on the top-right side of your head. Don't worry about it too much. Just do whatever you can with it.

Tie it off with a hair band and decorate it with a ribbon. Then take a comb and tease the gathered hair until it shifts around easily. Again, there's no need to obsess. Just do what you can.

If you put a little hairspray on it, it'll look a little better. And you're done!!

Continued on the right-hand page

AFTERWORD

Trinity Raven! I came up with them at the last moment. Originally the ones who were going to stand between our heroes and Jellal were Shô, Simon, and the others. But while I was writing the chapters of Erza's past (the chapters toward the end of the last volume), I started feeling really sorry for them. Even if Natsu and Gray were to defeat them, it wouldn't really solve their conflicts. And so, all very quickly, I set up the Trinity Raven. The scene of the fight between Natsu and Wally and Millianna was done in a very comical way, so it didn't draw the same kind of sympathy that my original idea had.

People who read these Afterword sections might have come to notice already, but tales like this change an awful lot. It happens all the time that a story I've completely thought through will take an unexpected turn. In this particular story arc, there have been a number of changes. The Trinity Raven is just a typical example. And my style is to not think too much about what comes after, so every week I find myself saying, *I wonder what will come next?* (Or, *what'll I do now?!!*) That's the way I am, but here, I actually have given the way this story arc ends a lot of thought. Well, I gave it a bit of vague thought on all the other stories. (sweat, sweat) For the end of the Deliora story arc, I thought, *Gray'll end up winning...right?* For the Phantom arc, *Makarov will prove to be really strong...right?* I sort of muddle through to the end.

But not this time!! I've given the end of this story arc some concrete thought!!! And it looks like it will turn out to be a really good story... At least I hope it turns out good...So expect great things!!

About the Creator

HIRO MASHIMA was born May 3, 1977, in the Nagano prefecture. His series *Rave Master* has made him one of the most popular manga artists in America. *Fairy Tail*, currently being serialized in *Weekly Shōnen Magazine*, is his latest creation.

Translation Notes

Japanese is a tricky language for most Westerners, and translation is often more art than science. For your edification and reading pleasure, here are notes on some of the places where we could have gone in a different direction in our translation of the work, or where a Japanese cultural reference is used.

General Notes:
Wizard

In the original Japanese version of *Fairy Tail*, you'll find panels in which the English word "wizard" is part of the original illustration. So this translation has taken that as its inspiration and translated the word *madōshi* as "wizard." But *madōshi*'s meaning is similar to certain Japanese words that have been borrowed by the English language, such as judo (the soft way) and kendo (the way of the sword). *Madō* is the way of magic, and *madōshi* are those who follow the way of magic. So although the word "wizard" is used in the original dialogue, a Japanese reader would be likely to think not of traditional Western wizards, such as Merlin or Gandalf, but of martial artists.

Names

Hiro Mashima has graciously agreed to provide official English spellings for just about all of the characters in *Fairy Tail*. Because this version of *Fairy Tail* is the first publication of most of these spellings, there will inevitably be differences between these spellings and some of the fan interpretations that may have spread throughout the Web or in other fan circles. Rest assured that the spellings contained in this book are the spellings that Mashima-sensei wanted for *Fairy Tail*.

Tama Gonzaburo, page iv

The Japanese word for "egg" is *tamago*. So Tama Gonzaburo is something of a pun on the word "egg."

Sneezing when someone is gossiping about you, page 27

There is an old saying that when you sneeze, someone is talking about you. This has turned into a shorthand version of a standard joke in Japanese TV dramas, anime, manga, and other media. A group of people are talking about a character, then there is a sudden scene change to that character who sneezes and wonders if he is coming down with a cold. In reality, very few people believe this is true, but the joke still "plays" nonetheless.

AH-CHOO!

In-cat-ceration Tube, page 31

The Japanese word for "incarceration" or "restraint" is *kôsoku*, and the Japanese word for "cat" is *neko*. Millianna's attack in Japanese was, *Ne-kôsoku* Tube (with "tube" being in English). Since there was no way to translate the pun on the manga page, I replaced it with an English pun and elected to explain it here in the notes.

The names in Trinity Raven, page 42

Vidaldus-han? Do I sense cowardice?

TEEHEE

All of the names of the members of Trinity Raven are Japanese words for birds. As you, the reader, have probably already guessed, *fukuro* is the Japanese word for "owl." Slightly less obvious are *taka*, which means "hawk," and *ikaruga*, which is the word used when referring to a bird known as the Japanese grosbeak.

Vidaldus-han, page 50

Japanese grosbeak speaks in the Kyoto version of the *Kansai-ben* dialect (accent for the *Kansai* region that mainly consists of Kobe, Osaka, Kyoto, and Nara but also includes the surrounding areas). In many versions of the *Kansai* accent of Japanese, the honorific *-san* is pronounced *-han*.

Faakin' Gals, page 72

Okay, I chickened out a little and transliterated (put the Japanese pronunciation intact in the alphabet) rather than translated Vidaldus's line. But there are reasons for it. The F-bomb has a certain amount of emotional content in English that it doesn't have in Japanese. In Japanese, it's just something that heavy-metal rockers or tough guys in movies say. While at the same time, the Japanese "swear words" being used in *Fairy Tail* are all rather tame—they might be said on TV without anyone batting an eye. Any Japanese equivalent to the F-bomb would be out of place in the Japanese version, and the actual F-bomb would be out of place in the American version.

Lock and rock, page 76

As any first-year Japanese language course will tell you, the Japanese people (who don't have training in the English language) cannot hear the difference between the *l* and *r* sounds. For example, the words "correction" and "collection" sound exactly the same to a Japanese native speaker. (The same kind of thing goes both ways. Native English speakers, at first, have a tough time distinguishing between the short and long vowels of Japanese words. "Mr. Oka," *Oka-san*, sounds very much like the Japanese word for "mother,"

okaa-san.) To a native Japanese speaker, "lock" and "rock" sound exactly the same and are spelled the same in Japanese.

Shampooing every morning, page 78

There is some research to back up Vidaldus's claim. Reportedly, daily washing strips the scalp of a beneficial oil called sebum, and can damage hair. Apparently the scalp tries to compensate for the washed-off oil by producing more oil, but breaking the daily shampooing habit will, within a little while, cause the scalp to return to its normal oil production, and one's hair will not be as greasy as it will seem when one first breaks the habit. At least one dermatologist recommends shampooing only twice or three times a week.

Water Cane, page 88

If you're wondering why a stick that helps people walk is thought of as a weapon, remember that in parts of Asia, caning is a still form of criminal punishment. It is used much like a whip, meant to flay skin off the caning victim's back. Often in Japanese period dramas, the villains will capture a hero or innocent bystander and cane him or her to try to get information.

Drainage Ditch, page 125

By the side of nearly every road in Japan is a drainage ditch to drain rain water from the road. The ditches are usually covered by small blocks of concrete, but in many rural and some urban settings, the ditches remain uncovered and present something of a hazard to pedestrians since many (if not most) of Japanese streets lack sidewalks.

Planc and plinc, page 155

This is supposed to be the sound of a samisen playing traditional music in the background. But since the samisen isn't a common instrument in the West, the sound effect doesn't come across as well as it does to Japanese readers.

Does it stare at you?…Within the fog bank, page 167

This verse is in the form of a haiku, the form of Japanese poetry that is best known to the Western world. It is descended from the older Japanese poem form, *waka*. But haiku is a form that is more bound by rules (it must be a natural setting; it must have some word indicating the season; etc.), and it is a shorter form of poem at seventeen syllables (5-7-5) to *waka*'s thirty-one (5-7-5-7-7). Although one can generally say more using seventeen syllables of English than one can in seventeen syllables of Japanese, language translation generally takes more words to get the point across—so with some imagination, one can translate haiku into the same number of syllables.

Preview of Volume 12

We're pleased to present you with a preview from volume 12. Please check our website (www.delreymanga.com) to see when this volume will be available in English. For now you'll have to make do with Japanese!

TOMARE!

止まれ

[STOP!]

You're going the wrong way!

Manga is a completely different type of reading experience.

To start at the *beginning*, go to the *end*!

That's right! Authentic manga is read the traditional Japanese way—from right to left, exactly the *opposite* of how American books are read. It's easy to follow: Just go to the other end of the book and read each page—and each panel—from right side to left side, starting at the top right. Now you're experiencing manga as it was meant to be!

W9-AQI-214